Serendipitous Heartbreak

Jenala Jones

BookLeaf Publishing

India | USA | UK

Presentation by *BookLeaf Publishing*

Web: www.bookleafpub.com

E-mail: info@bookleafpub.com

ISBN - 9789357447928

First edition 2021

To all who have felt lost or broken, yet are
doing all they can to carry on.

ACKNOWLEDGEMENT

A huge thank you to all of my family for being an inspiration for several poems in this book and providing continuous support from the early stages of my writing career. Thank you to my dear mother, Jennifer Jones, for sharing an equal passion for writing. Thank you to my beautiful sisters, Miyannah, Leah, Bo, and Elianna Jones for being amazing cheerleaders for me to reach my dreams.

An incredible thank you to my dear friends for lending a listening ear and showing up to support me at live performances. Thank you to my big brother Zachariah Bradley, for always believing in me and helping keep my creative batteries charged. Thank you to one of my closest friends, my soulmate, Bernadette Wong, for being an incredible audience and for giving me honest opinions about my work. Also, thank you for your contribution to the work of 'Cyche'. Thank you to one of my best friends, my soul sister, Erica Luckett, for the unwavering support and encouragement to write more frequently and building my confidence as a writer.

Thank you to past and present coworkers and colleagues for believing in my work, providing me with strength and comfort along my journey, as well as being a strong supporter of my passion. Also, thank you to BookLeaf Publishing for the opportunity and means of developing this book.

Thank you to one of my biggest influencers and inspirations, BTS, for helping me strengthen and maintain the drive I needed to achieve each goal I set. Thank you for the unwavering love and care, as well as the sincerity and authenticity within your own work that has helped mold me into the writer I am today.

Finally, thank you to my amazing and loving furry companion, Vinnie, for carrying me through, sitting through every at home performance, and listening to every rough draft without objection.

Sincerely, I thank you all.

Reflection

What lessons can truly be learned without
looking within,
to experience and understand
the emotions and thoughts that reside there?

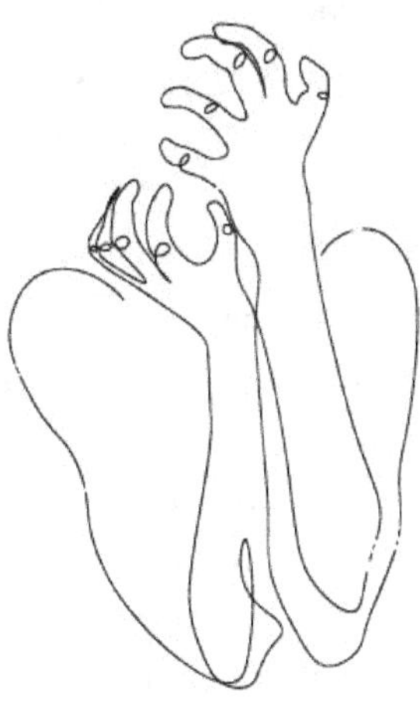

Ease

It was so easy.
So easy to spend time with you.
Hours would pass as we watched movie after
movie.
More hours would pass before I realized you've
slept through them all.

It was so easy.
So easy to talk to you.
To tell you the deepest parts of myself without
the worry of shame or judgement,
just knowing you'd still love me the same.

It was so easy.
So easy to make you angry.
Arguing for hours on end about things that now
have no meaning or purpose.
Grateful we gained such clarity together.

It is so hard.
So hard to believe that I gained such a
substantial amount of luck, enough to intertwine
our paths forever.

It is so hard.
So hard to imagine my life without you.

The weightlessness and freedom your presence
grants me,
makes it impossible to comprehend a life on the
ground.

It is so hard.
So hard to love anyone else,
as easily as I love you.

Rainy Mornings

I wake up to a gray sky.
Turning, I attempt to grasp onto consciousness.

I fight memories
Of the dreams that tormented me throughout the
night.

I breathe in, and out
Again, and again
As I try to ignore the anxieties lying inside me.

Listening to the persistent,
Rhythmic dance
Of the branches on my window.

I open my eyes once more to a gray sky.
Allowing the rain to wash me away.

Cyche

My life is so bleak,
Can't be mad,
Because it might turn to shit.

Was this what I imagined,
Can't be sane,
Really thought there'd be more coursing through
my veins.

Had I perished at the hands of anguish,
Would I be happy for this self-directed malice?
To have been freed of my current sufferings?

Gripping my neck, wringing my reality,
Enmity building with censured mentions.
Words spilling from the mouth
I trusted most.

My own.
Mind betraying me,
Emotions escaping me,
Behavior construing me.

At least,
In the odd hours of the night,
In which this has become the only time I sleep,

My eyes close to the opening,
Of a congenial world.
A world that is my own yet,
I am free from myself.

Hurt

Ignoring the pain will not heal the wound.

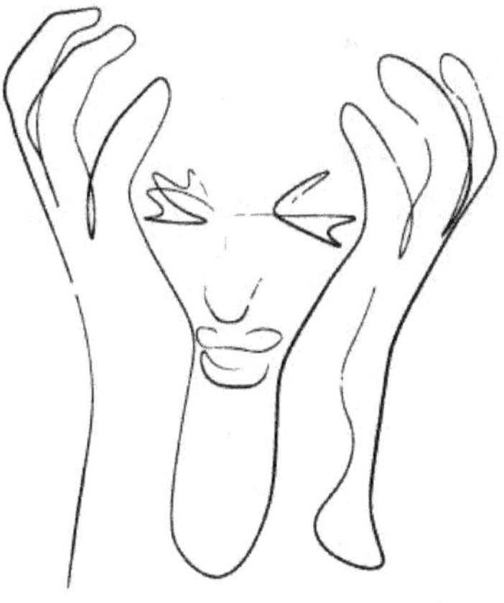

Perhaps

Perhaps it's better
To build up new walls and reinforce the ones
built years ago.

Perhaps it's better
To rip out my own heart and trap it inside the
safe built within the depths of my chest,
Safe away from the world.

Perhaps it's better
To place distance between us or restrain the need
to be around you.

Perhaps it's better
To allow my insecurities to be free so that they
stop me before it's too late.

Perhaps it's better
To be the cause of my own pain so that I hate
myself instead of you.

Numb

I guess numb is a feeling too.

When you know things are important, but
nothing feels important.

When basic necessities just don't feel necessary.

When anxiety ridden chores or tasks no longer
rule over your heart.

When your favorite people or favorite things that
used to make you smile, just don't.

When you smile and laugh, but know how
forced it all is.

When delicious food no longer holds flavor.

When the sunshine doesn't give you motivation.

When you don't feel like Superman, or super
anything.

When you love deeply, but don't see the point in
the end.

Well I guess, numb is a feeling, too.

Loss

Grief can bring powerful awakenings, along with the realization that you are much stronger than you think.

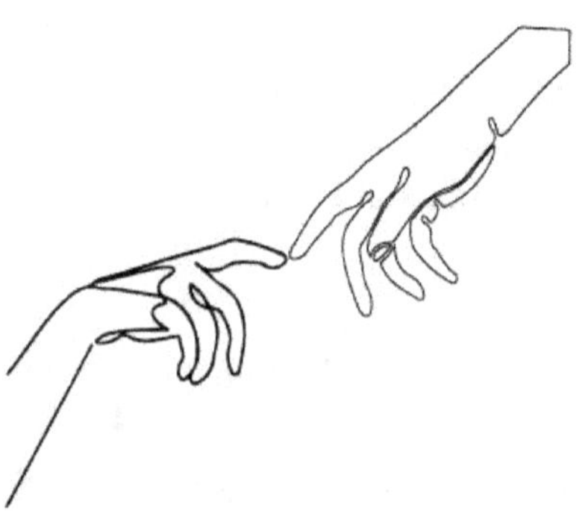

I Love You

I love you.
Three words I always considered overused,
Yet never used enough.

I love you.
Something I wish I didn't wait so long to say.
And I promise to say it everyday going forward.

I love you.
Something I had always imagined I'd whisper to you,
On my wedding day as you walked beside me.

I love you.
Three words I wish I could've said,
Before I lost you.

Promises

I'm getting really tired of your broken promises.
Promises telling me you'd call
on this day at this time.
Having me wait
excitedly
anxiously
desperately.
For something that was never to come.

I'm getting really tired of your broken promises.
Promises telling me that we'd get together real
soon,
for lunch
for shopping
for movie dates.
Getting me hyped for trivial things I don't
normally care for,
just because I'd be spending these moments,
with you.

No, I'm not the one,
who needs your money to feel like I haven't
been forgotten.

No, I'm not the one

who needs material things over the presence of
your physical being.

No, I'm not the one
who is dependent on the success of this
relationship to feel confident and guilt-free.

Whether you do, or you don't,
don't try to blame anyone else for your own
neglect.

Whether you will, or you won't,
won't matter in the end if you're unable to own
up to your mistakes.

Whether you can, or you can't,
can't stop me from living the life that has been
fatefully written for me.

Either way,
Baby, I'll be alright.

Absence

Pure, contemporary, cocoa eyes
Locking mine,
Entrapping me in an eternal hold.
One that I can't imagine breaking free from.

Fitting flawlessly,
In my arms.
I gaze as she sleeps,
As she eats.
Soon

Speaking to me with
Words neither of us fully understand.
Our connection growing,
Stronger with each random syllable.

Soft, stubby fingers
Contrasting with my lengthy, calloused ones.
Allowing me to slowly guide her
Around and
Around in small circles
Not to overwhelm her inexperienced legs.

Tensions build, as time ticks on.
Forces objecting, rejecting me
As my daughter talks,

As my daughter walks
Further from me.

Confused and unaware
Of the power I hold
To keep her close.
Oblivious to what will be the outcome of my
yield.

Now
She has grown.
Up and on
Without me
Despite me.
I watch her closely
From a distance.

Birthdays, graduations,
Happy days, sad days
Passing me like the city buses do.
My feet
Not knowing how, too nerve stricken to
Move forward
Thus making me miss my chance
Every time.
Reminding me of the void,
The punishment I feel
Is well deserved for abandoning a bond
I swore to.

This is what's best.
My absence is necessary.
What good is a phone call?
A lame attempt to connect...

If only I knew
That'd be all I needed.
If only I knew
That'd be all she needed,
To be reminded
That what we've built,
All those years ago,
Is not something
That could ever truly be broken.

Anger

Constant exasperation is a sign for you to change your environment- or the people in it.

Harvest

You made the decision on your own,
Not to trust me.
You made up your mind,
To believe your insecurities.
You made the choice,
To let the words of others convince you.

You opted to wait on me,
Without telling me where to meet you.
You chose to leave me,
When I needed you the most.
You assumed neglect,
While I experienced it head on by the hands of
your demons.

You settled to lie and manipulate.
Actions I find hard to forgive.
So now, reap the seeds you sowed,
In the loneliness you've feared all along.

Fool

You dare to touch me.
Skin, purer than the rawest of emeralds.
In other words, unworthy of a graze by your
hand.
You dare to call my name.
Having it slip from your tongue like syrup
Intending it to sound like sweet reassurance.
Yet all I hear is sour, toxic,
Bullshit.

The lines you feed to my friends,
As if they're gullible enough to gobble up
The lies and insecurities.
Yet you forget, they are my friends.
My sisters who have been and will be
By my side through the deadliest of storms.

You dare to look at me.
Your eyes taking me in hungrily, desperately,
Hoping that with enough drinks I will
Relax enough to dance with you.
You dare to stand in my presence.
How bold you are.

Know that I don't forgive easily.
Know that I don't forget.
Know that you won't ever get the chance.

Growth

Seemingly the most torturing and
uncomfortable, yet healthy and freeing thing a
person can strive for is personal growth.

Kinky

Early on,
I felt unsure.
"Which way do I go?
Straight? Smooth?
Or is it ok to travel in circles?
To be big, and voluminous?"

Honestly,
I've always preferred the latter.
Plus, my girl didn't seem
to mind at all.
She'd let me do as I pleased.

Through the years though, that started to change.
My girl,
She started restricting me.
Pulling me this way and that,
Tying me down,
Only to free me
In the late or early hours of the day.
Exhausting.

But I guess,
This was around the time I noticed.
More eyes on my girl and me.
The prolonged stares causing my girl

To shyly tuck me behind her ear.
To flatten me down against her scalp.

Years go by.
Cuts,
chemical treatments,
pins and clips.
Me, ignoring her stubbornness
while she,
ignores my pride,
Desperate attempts to tame me.
Exhausting.

So much confusion,
Frustration,
Anger.
400° is enough to make anyone go frizzy after,
am I wrong?

These days
Oh, how I've grown.
It's been awhile
Since my girl tucked
Me behind her ear too,
Not that I give her much choice.

Now,
When we get those looks,
She gives me a flip and a toss.

Allowing me to stretch out
and wave to my fans.
She brushes me out instead of down.

Yes, traveling in
Casual, carefree, coils
Will always beat that restraint
of having to fall in line.
Watch,
My girl and I will show you.
Kinky is the new convention.

Ready, Set..

Quiet.
Not much other than distant chatter behind my
door.
Focused.
I breathe deeply again and again to calm my
thoughts.
Slowly.
I open my eyes, staring deeply into my
reflection.

Knock.
Twice, softly, hoping to kindly alert me from the
other side.
Time.
Is now, so I rise making my way out into the
hall.
Walk.
But not too slow or else I'd miss the cue and my
chance to..

Breathe.
Deeper now and more panicked as I try to calm
my nerves.

Smile.
To reassure the director, to reassure myself.

Remember.
All of the auditions and rehearsals leading to this
moment finally allowing me to…

Shine.
Bright, as the spotlight ignites me.

Acceptance

Rarely will you have control of everything, but
you will always have the power to decide the
best way to move forward.

Reflective Point of View

Pushing back the longer strands of hair that coil
to tickle the forehead.
The same forehead that grows wrinkles and
creases once confused or angry.

Hickory eyes wide, curious pupils, taking in
every feature.
The same eyes that shrink into oblivion,
crinkling at their sides when entertained.

Nose begins its performance of a wriggle and
flare once the eyes give it attention.
The same nose that took extra care smelling
each blooming blossom this past spring.

Lips, full at rest, become thin when stretched
over an array of large white nacreous teeth.
Delicate craters piercing either side.
The same teeth that have been kept hidden due
to a smile lacking sincerity, until recently.

Battle scars from the adolescent war remain.
Just a reminder of all that's been overcome.
Age spots, beauty marks glitter the warm tones
of the skin,
A confetti of growth and memories.

Taking in these few, yet dominant, details of
your own reflection, finally only one word
comes to mind.

Beautiful.

I am

I am powerful.
Yet, I am not a mind reader.

I am nurturing.
Yet, I am not a mother.

I am self-less.
Yet, I refuse to put anyone before myself.

I am loyal.
Yet, I know when to walk away.

I am resilient.
Yet, I will not allow repeated offenses.

I am clingy.
Yet, I will not hesitate to let you go.

Tree

The wind blows harshly.
The leaves of the tree shake and wave like a flag
of surrender.
Some aren't strong enough to withstand the
blow and fall into the breeze.

The wind blows agonizingly.
The branches shift and bend.
Moving in ways to avoid breaking.
Desperate and determined to hold on.

The wind blows mockingly.
The trunk is unmoving and unbothered.
Deeply rooted in confidence, faith, and inner
strength.
Not phased by the games of the wind.
Not afraid of possible damage the wind could
bring with it.
Because no matter what, it will always stand
strong.

I am a tree.